Taj Mahal

India's Majestic Tomb

By Linda Tagliaferro

Consultant: Stephen F. Brown, Director
Institute of Medieval Philosophy and Theology, Boston College

BEARPORT
PUBLISHING COMPANY, INC.

New York, New York

Credits

Cover, Adam Woolfitt / CORBIS; title page, Adam Woolfitt / CORBIS

Background images (throughout), Mary Evans Picture Library; 4-5, Peter Bowater / Alamy Images; 5, Dinodia Picture Agency, Bombay, India; / www.bridgeman.co.uk; 7, Victoria & Albert Museum, London / Art Resource, NY; 8, Mary Evans Picture Library; 9, Mughal Emperor Akbar (c.1605) (centre) Symbolically Passing the Crown from His Son Jahangir to his Grandson Shah Jahan (1627-1658) c.1630 (vellum), Bichtir (fl. 1620) / © The Trustees of the Chester Beatty Library, Dublin, / www.bridgeman.co.uk; 10, Portrait of Arjumand Banu Begum (d.1631) Mumtaz-i Mahal, Indian School / Private Collection, Dinodia Picture Agency, Bombay, India; / www.bridgeman.co.uk; 11, Shah Jahan (1592-1666) and Muntaz Mahal, his wife (d.1629), Mughal, / Private Collection, / www.bridgeman.co.uk; 12, POPPERFOTO / Alamy; 13, Enzo & Paolo Ragazzini / CORBIS; 14-15, Bridgeman Art Library, London / www.bridgeman.co.uk; 15 (top), The Ancient Art & Architecture Collection; 15 (bottom), Dinodia Photo Library; 16-17, The Art Archive; 18, Emperor Khurram (Shah Jahan), with attendants, Mughal, / Private Collection./ www.bridgeman.co.uk; 18-19, Borromeo / Art Resource, NY; 20-21(both), British Library Images Online; 22-23 (both), Mary Evans Picture Library; 24-25, Dinodia Photo Library; 26, Dinodia Photo Library; 26-27, Rodica Prato; 29, Adam Woolfitt / CORBIS.

Design and production by Dawn Beard Creative, Triesta Hall of Blu-Design, and Octavo Design and Production, Inc.

Library of Congress Cataloging-in-Publication Data

Tagliaferro, Linda.
  Taj Mahal: India's majestic tomb / by Linda Tagliaferro; consultant, Stephen Brown.
    p. cm. — (Castles, palaces & tombs)
  Includes bibliographical references and index.
  ISBN 1-59716-004-0 (lib. bdg.)—ISBN 1-59716-027-X (pbk.)
  1. Taj Mahal (Agra, India)—Juvenile literature. I. Title. II. Series.

  DS486.A3T32 2005
  954'.2—dc22

2004020991

For more information, write to Bearport Publishing Company, Inc., 101 Fifth Avenue, Suite 6R, New York, New York 10003. Printed in the United States of America.

1 2 3 4 5 6 7 8 9 10

Table of Contents

The Saddest Day

Shah Jahan (SHA juh-HAHN) was not expecting the bad news. His wife had just given birth to their fourteenth child, a girl. He was told that the baby was healthy and his wife was resting. A few hours later, his wife called for him. She was dying.

The Taj Mahal

On June 17, 1631, she closed her eyes for the last time. Shah Jahan was sadder than he had ever been in his life. He decided to build a magnificent **tomb** for his wife. It would be called the Taj Mahal (TODGE muh-HAHL).

Shah Jahan and his wife

Taj Mahal means
"Crown Palace."

The Mighty Moguls

A long time ago, Shah Jahan was a powerful and rich **emperor** of the land that is now India. His father and grandfather had the throne before him. This royal family was known as the **Mogul** emperors. They ruled for hundreds of years.

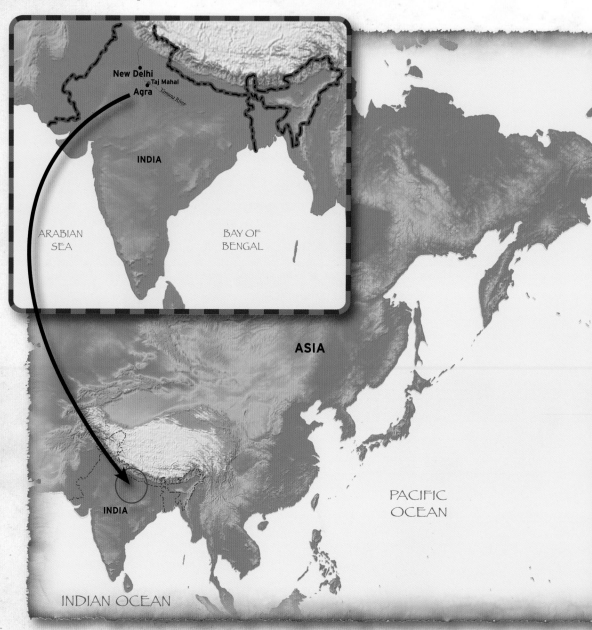

Shah Jahan loved art, jewels, and fancy buildings. He decided that the Taj Mahal would be one of the most expensive places in the world. It would be built of shiny white marble and decorated with **diamonds** and **rubies**.

Shah Jahan seated on the Peacock Throne

NORTH AMERICA

ATLANTIC OCEAN

Shah Jahan owned the Peacock Throne. This royal chair was decorated with hundreds of jewels.

A Joyous Birth

Before Shah Jahan became emperor, he had another name. When he was born in 1592, his grandfather named him Khurram (khuh-RAM). This name means "joyous." As Khurram grew, his grandfather taught him how to become a great **ruler**.

Khurram's grandfather arrives in Surat, India.

Khurram loved to hear his grandfather's stories. He heard all about the battles he'd won. He enjoyed learning how to hunt from him, too. Sadly, when Khurram was 13, his grandfather died. Then his father became emperor.

Khurram's grandfather (center) passing the crown to his son, Khurram's father

Khurram's grandfather, Akbar (OCK-bar), rode an elephant when he led his armies in battle.

A Great Love

When Khurram was 16, he met a beautiful young woman named Arjumand Banu Begum (ARE-joo-MOND Buh-NOO Beh-GUM). He fell in love and asked his father if he could marry her. The answer was yes. They had to wait, however, until the emperor's wise men picked a day they thought to be lucky.

Arjumand Banu Begum

Five years later, the couple married. To honor Arjumand, Khurram's father called her Mumtaz Mahal (MOOM-taz muh-HAHL). In 1627, Khurram's father became ill and died. Khurram then became emperor and changed his name to Shah Jahan. Shah Jahan was afraid that his brothers would try to **overthrow** him, so he had them killed.

Shah Jahan and his wife, Mumtaz Mahal

Mumtaz Mahal means the "Chosen One of the Palace." Shah Jahan means "King of the World."

Treasures from Afar

Shah Jahan searched for the best **designers** for his wife's tomb. It was to be built in Agra, the capital of the Mogul empire. **Architects** from India, Persia, and other lands presented ideas. The emperor finally chose a team of 37 people to design the building.

Throughout the twentieth century, elephants helped people work in some countries. These elephants are helping carry logs that have just been cut.

small city was built outside Agra.
0 workers.
e than 20 years. One thousand
marble from far-off places. Rare
rom the Indian Ocean. Jewels used
as far away as China.

This Indian elephant is learning how to work.

Shah Jahan wanted a tomb like the Taj Mahal for his own resting place. It was to be all black, but it was never built.

A Shining Building

The Taj Mahal has a large garden surrounded by tall red walls and rows of trees. Four narrow waterways cut through the garden. In the garden's center is a large pool. In its water, you can see the **reflection** of the white building's onion-shaped **dome**. Four towers, each 200 feet high, stand at each corner of the main building.

The Mogul emperors were Muslims. Their religion **inspired** the Taj Mahal. Since four is a **holy** number, the garden has four main parts. Inside the tomb, black marble letters on the walls spell out writing from the **Koran**.

The walls inside the Taj Mahal were beautifully designed.

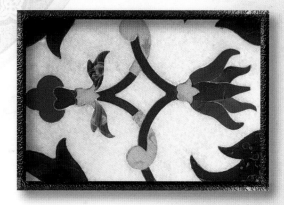

If someone makes a sound under the dome of the Taj Mahal, it can echo for 12 seconds or more.

Heaven on Earth

The Taj Mahal was more than just a tomb. It was also a place where people could honor Mumtaz Mahal. At times, Shah Jahan had his throne brought to the gardens. There he sat, remembering his wife.

People enjoying the gardens at the Taj Mahal

During Shah Jahan's rule, peacocks and songbirds lived in the gardens of the Taj Mahal.

Shah Jahan allowed members of his court to spend time there. The gardens were like a **paradise**. People listened to the quiet, flowing water of the fountains. They feasted on wonderful food and drink.

A New Emperor

As Shah Jahan got older, he became ill. Each of his sons wanted to be the new emperor. Only one could take the throne. The sons battled one another. The youngest son, Aurangzeb (OAR-ang-ZEHB), fought hardest and won. He killed his brothers and put his own son in prison.

Shah Jahan with his servants

The Red Fort

Aurangzeb moved his father into the Red **Fort**. Shah Jahan was not allowed out. Every day, he looked across the land to see the Taj Mahal. He longed to visit his wife's tomb. He, however, never got the chance. Eight years later, Shah Jahan died. He was buried next to his wife.

In 1565, Akbar built the great Red Fort in Agra. It was built to protect his family and others against enemies.

British Rule

The Mogul emperors ruled until the 1800s. Then the British got control of India. They took over the Taj Mahal and all the other Mogul buildings. British soldiers used the gardens for picnics. They littered the Taj Mahal's courtyard and the rest of the grounds.

Sir Harry Smith and his soldiers, during the Battle of Moodkee in 1848, as the British fight for control of India

The British didn't seem to care what happened to this beautiful place. They held large parties on the marble terrace. Some visitors stole jewels from the walls. The gardens filled with weeds. Soon, the Taj Mahal lost much of its beauty.

The British storm a city in India

Under British rule, India was called the Raj. This word means "kingdom" in an Indian language.

Saving the Tomb

In the 1830s, a British governor of India, Lord Bentinck, came along. He decided to destroy the Taj Mahal and other Mogul buildings. He wanted to take the expensive marble and send it to England. There, rich people could buy the marble to decorate their houses.

Lord Bentinck

The Taj Mahal's original gates were made from silver. They were stolen in the 1700s.

The first building torn down was a fort in Delhi. Workers took all the marble and shipped it to England. Surprisingly, however, few people were interested in buying the marble. Lord Bentinck decided not to tear down any more buildings. The Taj Mahal was saved.

An illustration of the Taj Mahal in 1840

Restoring the Taj Mahal

Lord Curzon was a British governor in India in the 1900s. He was a fan of Indian art. He loved the Taj Mahal and **restored** it to its glory. Artists decorated the walls with diamonds and rubies. Workers polished the white marble building until it gleamed.

In the gardens, workers planted trees and colorful flowers. They filled the pools with water from the Yamuna River. The soft sound of water fountains once again filled the air. Today, the Taj Mahal delights visitors with all the beauty of its first days.

A view of the Taj Mahal from the Yamuna River

In 1803, an **earthquake** shook the Taj Mahal and made cracks in the towers. Lord Curzon's workers also repaired these cracks.

Visiting the Taj Mahal

To visit the Taj Mahal today, you first need to take an airplane to New Delhi, the capital of India. From there, you take a two-hour train ride north to the city of Agra. Then you can take a bus to the tomb.

After a short drive, you arrive at the gatehouse. As you follow the guide through the gate, you will see a magnificent building beyond the beautiful gardens. After a long walk, you will finally reach the Taj Mahal.

One of four towers

Yamuna River

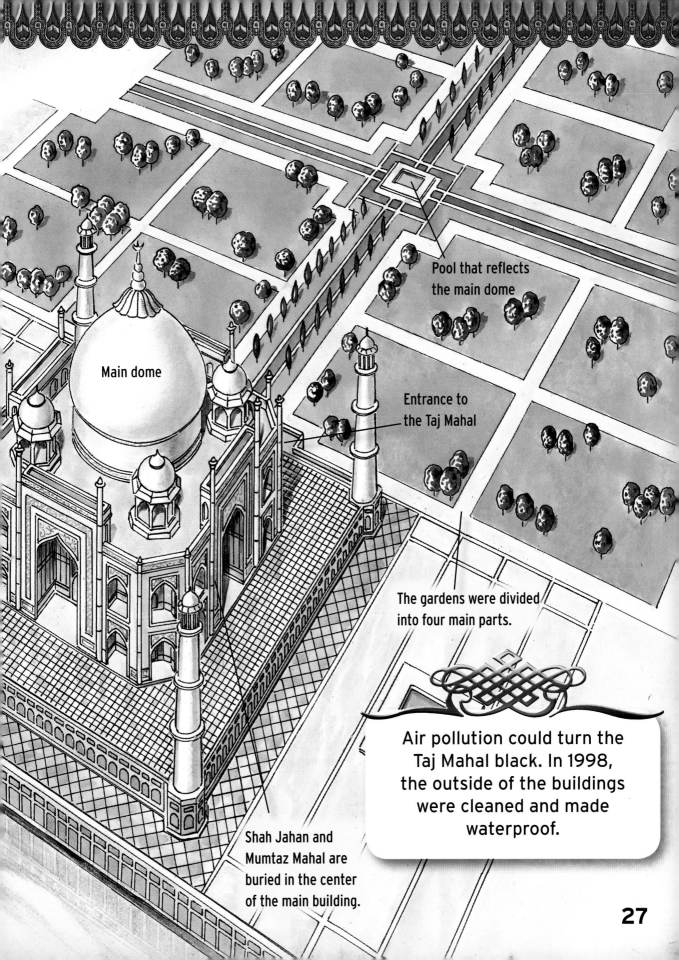

Main dome

Pool that reflects the main dome

Entrance to the Taj Mahal

The gardens were divided into four main parts.

Air pollution could turn the Taj Mahal black. In 1998, the outside of the buildings were cleaned and made waterproof.

Shah Jahan and Mumtaz Mahal are buried in the center of the main building.

Just the Facts

- The area of modern India is about one-third the size of the United States.

- Today, the word "mogul" can mean someone of great wealth or power.

- Muslim law said men could have four wives. Mumtaz Mahal was Shah Jahan's second, and favorite, wife.

- Forty-three kinds of gems were used to decorate the Taj Mahal.

- The Taj Mahal is taller than a 20-story building.

- Each of the Taj Mahal's four towers has 162 steps leading to its top.

- The Taj Mahal is open from sunrise until sunset every day except Friday.

- Visitors to the Taj Mahal must remove their shoes as a sign of respect.

Timeline

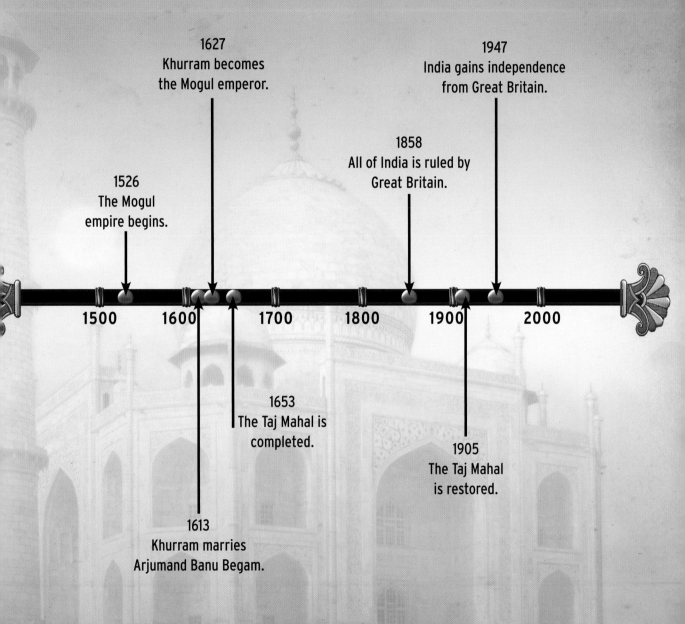

1627
Khurram becomes
the Mogul emperor.

1947
India gains independence
from Great Britain.

1858
All of India is ruled by
Great Britain.

1526
The Mogul
empire begins.

1500   1600   1700   1800   1900   2000

1653
The Taj Mahal is
completed.

1905
The Taj Mahal
is restored.

1613
Khurram marries
Arjumand Banu Begam.

Glossary

architects (AR-ki-tekts) people who design buildings and manage their construction

designers (di-ZINE-urz) people who plan and decorate rooms and their furnishings

diamonds (DYE-muhndz) hard precious stones that are usually colorless

dome (DOHM) a roof, shaped like half of a round globe

earthquake (URTH-*kwayk*) a sudden shaking of a part of the earth, caused by movement of the earth's crust

emperor (EM-pur-ur) the male ruler of an empire, or group of countries that have the same ruler

fort (FORT) a strong building that is used during battles for protection

holy (HOH-lee) having to do with God or religion

inspired (in-SPIRED) gave the idea or encouragement for

Koran (kor-AHN) the holy book of the Muslim religion

Mogul (MOH-guhl) related to the Muslim empire that ruled India from 1526–1857

overthrow (*oh*-vur-THROH) to remove a person from power by force

paradise (PA-ruh-*dise*) a place of great beauty, peace, and joy

reflection (ri-FLEKT-shun) an image of something on a shiny surface

restored (ri-STORD) something that is returned to its original condition

rubies (ROO-beez) valuable, red precious stones used in making jewelry

ruler (ROO-lur) someone who rules, or has power over, a country or countries

tomb (TOOM) a grave, room, or building in which a dead body is buried

Bibliography

Begley, W.E., and Z.A. Desai. *Taj Mahal — The Illumined Tomb.* Cambridge, MA: The Aga Khan Program for Islamic Architecture (1989).

Carroll, David. *The Taj Mahal.* New York, NY: Newsweek Book Division (1972).

Goodwin, William. *India (Modern Nations of the World.).* San Diego, CA: Lucent Books (2000).

Watson, Francis. *India — A Concise History.* New York, NY: Thames & Hudson (2002).

In addition, the author conducted a telephone interview with the information officer at the India Office of Tourism, New York City.

Read More

Arnold, Caroline. *The Taj Mahal.* Brookfield, CT: Millbrook Press (2004).

Marshall, Julia. *Shah Jahan and the Story of the Taj Mahal.* Washington, D.C.: Amideast Publications (1996).

Moorcroft, Christine. *The Taj Mahal (Great Buildings).* Austin, TX: Raintree Steck-Vaughn Company (1998).

Learn More Online

Visit these Web sites to learn more about the Taj Mahal:

http://rubens.anu.edu.au/student.projects/tajmahal/home.html

www.pbs.org/treasuresoftheworld/a_nav/taj_nav/main_tajfrm.html

www.taj-mahal.net

Index

About the Author

Linda Tagliaferro is an award-winning writer who is based
in Little Neck, New York. This is her 17th book for children.
She has also written for adults and young adults.